GODS OF INDIA

Indra Tests the Sage

SHUBHA VILAS

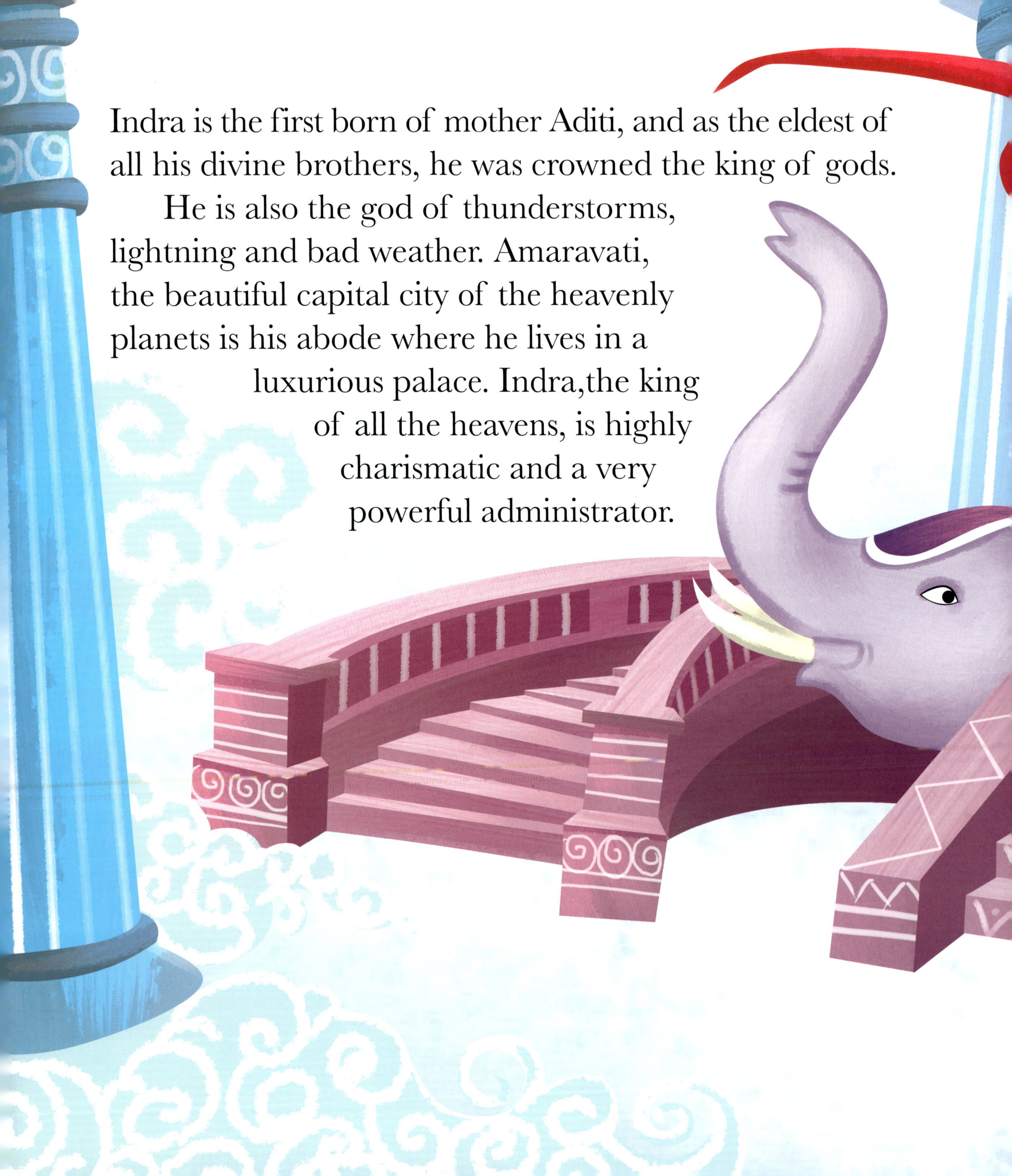

Indra is the first born of mother Aditi, and as the eldest of all his divine brothers, he was crowned the king of gods.

He is also the god of thunderstorms, lightning and bad weather. Amaravati, the beautiful capital city of the heavenly planets is his abode where he lives in a luxurious palace. Indra,the king of all the heavens, is highly charismatic and a very powerful administrator.

One thing that always bewildered Indra endlessly was how the sages and rishis were always absorbed in penance even in bad weather. There was one particular sage who did such severe austerities that nothing moved him, neither deadly thunderstorms nor harsh summers and winters.

Intrigued by him, Indra decided to test his mettle. What would it take to divert his mind? These were experiments he did occasionally to find out about human nature. There was one test in particular, which he had tried on many sages and he had never been disappointed.

Disguising himself as a king lost in the forest, he reached the sage's ashram. He found the sage deep in meditation. Sensing Indra's presence, the sage opened his eyes. On the pretext of having to answer nature's call, Indra handed over a shining, deleterious sword to the exalted sage.

Hesitant about handling a weapon of destruction, the sage asked the king of heavens to leave it inside his house. Indra used all his charms to convince the sage how precious his sword was and how priceless things need to be handled. Understanding how much Indra loved his sword, the sage relented and agreed to hold the sword for a few seconds. Indra left with a naughty smile on his lips, never to return. The sage patiently waited with the sword in his hands.

After a long wait, the sage's inquisitive mind began ticking. He turned the sword around and observed it keenly. Never had he seen a symbol of power like this, let alone hold one! This was no less than the imperial sword of Indra, the king of the demigods. It couldn't be ordinary. The glazing gems on the golden hilt of the shiny steel blade mesmerised the simple sage. His eyes scanned every inch of the wonder object he held in his hands. He was thoroughly impressed!

Wanting to experience first-hand the power of the sword that was in his grip, the sage gently swung the sword around and struck a log of wood that lay in a corner of his hermitage. To his amazement, one slight snick tore open the huge log. He was thrilled.

He now ventured out and began swishing the sword aimlessly, felling gigantic trees and cracking open massive boulders. He discovered joy in this newfound power of control.

The sage abandoned his hermitage and began wandering around looking for opportunities to exhibit his strength. Soon tigers, giant wolves, mad elephants, scavenging vultures and grizzly bears became his victims as he slashed their heads. Gone was the compassion, and gone was the hunger for spiritual pursuits. In place now was this fresh hunger for power and craving for adoration, wealth and prestige.

The sage soon morphed into a deadly dacoit. The forest became the hideout of a band of dacoits led by him. And it all started with him agreeing to hold that one sword for a few seconds!

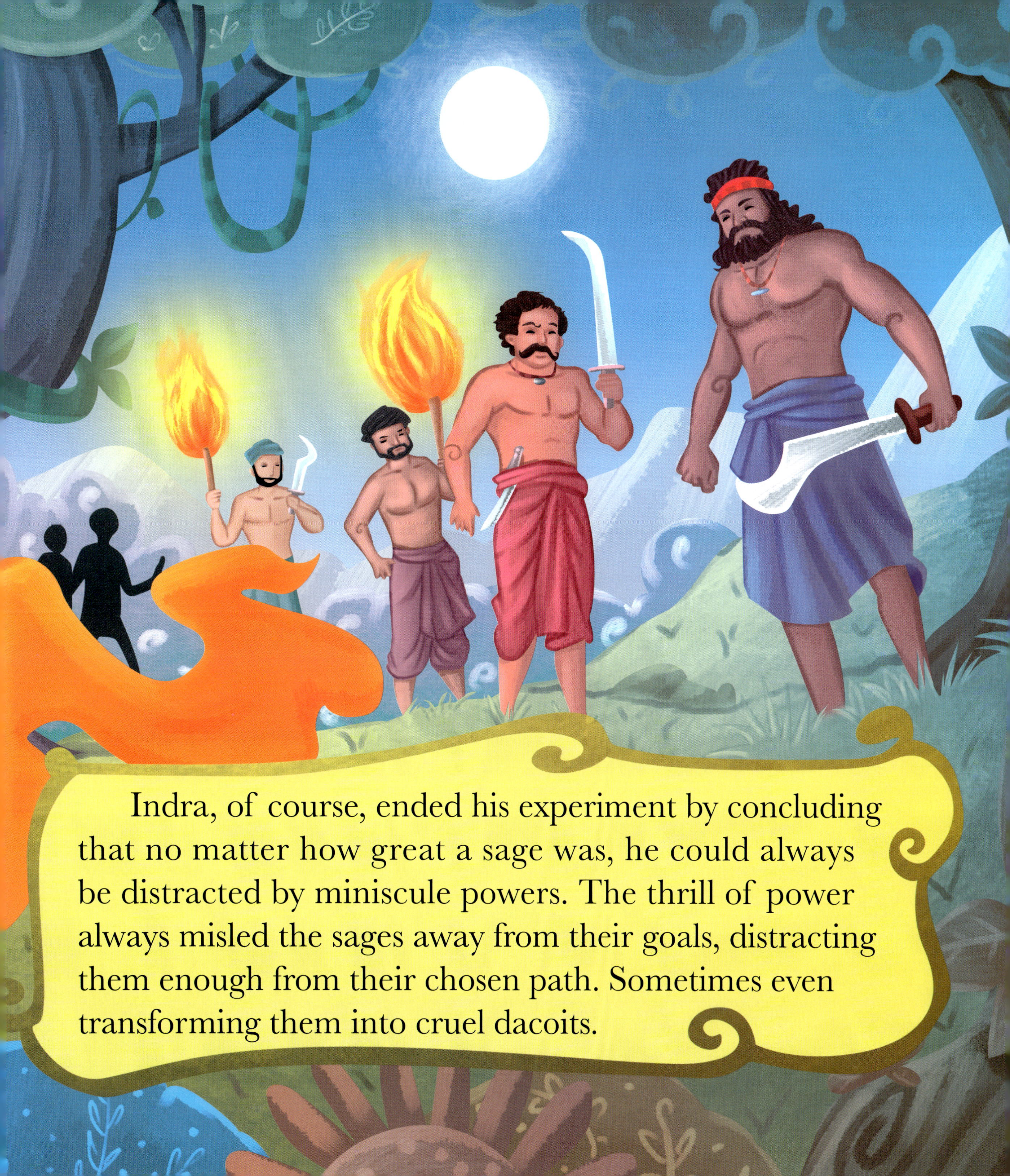

Indra, of course, ended his experiment by concluding that no matter how great a sage was, he could always be distracted by miniscule powers. The thrill of power always misled the sages away from their goals, distracting them enough from their chosen path. Sometimes even transforming them into cruel dacoits.

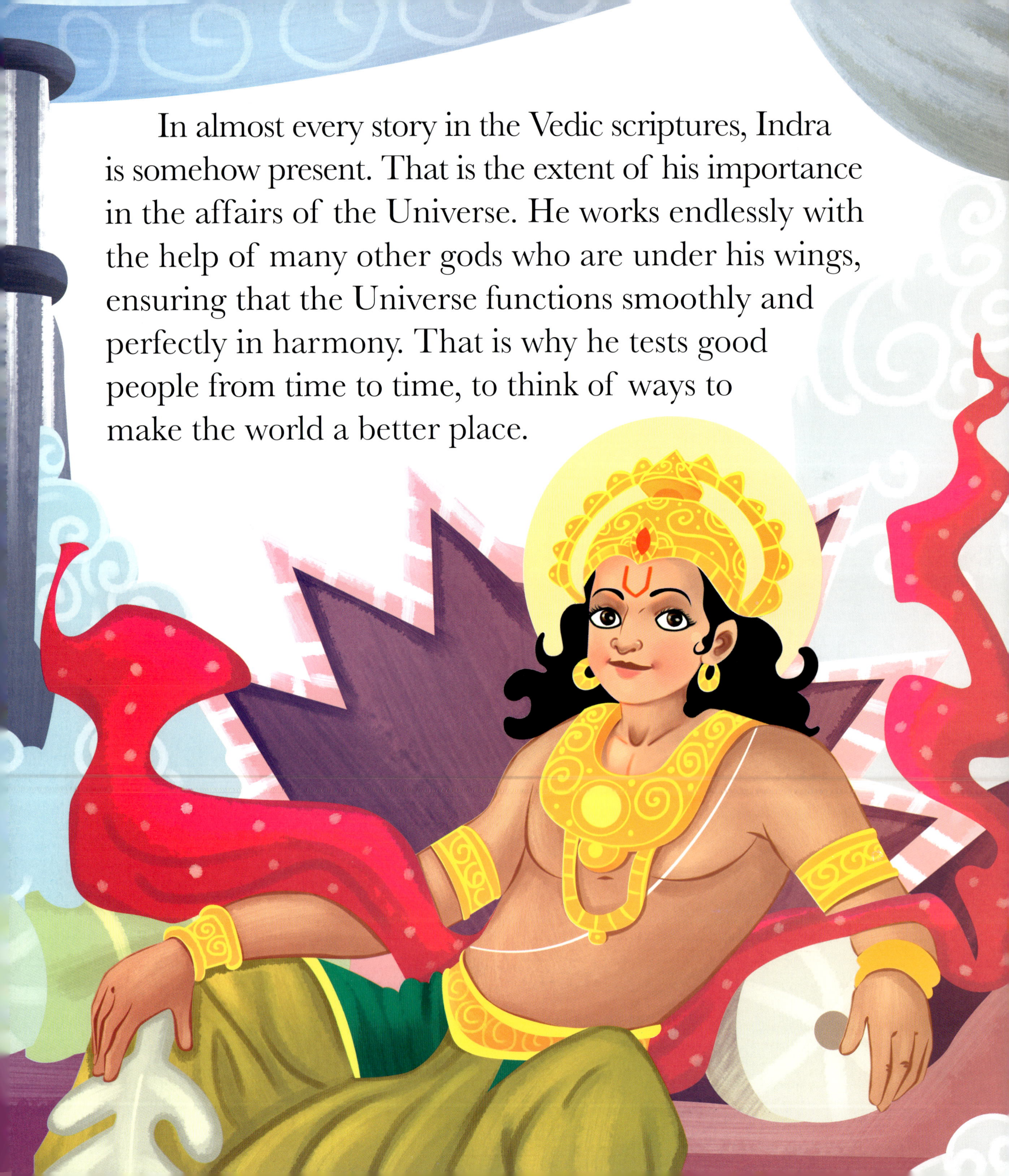

In almost every story in the Vedic scriptures, Indra is somehow present. That is the extent of his importance in the affairs of the Universe. He works endlessly with the help of many other gods who are under his wings, ensuring that the Universe functions smoothly and perfectly in harmony. That is why he tests good people from time to time, to think of ways to make the world a better place.